Genevieve Whitford

Queen Anne's Lace

and other poems

by

Genevieve Smith Whitford

Drawings by Roberta Froncek
Graphics by Tad Froncek

HARP PRESS
822 Magdeline Drive, Madison, Wisconsin 53704
Copyright 1982
ISBN 0-9610456-0-4
Third Printing

*We have art in order that we may not
perish from the truth.*

Nietzsche

Foreword

Queen Anne's Lace is a common weed, as pervasive, persistent, and familiar as the ideas and feelings expressed in this book. It is beautiful in its simplicity.

A poet once said that we write poetry because we have something to say, and no other way to say it. Most of these poems grew from an inner need to deal with ordinary human experience, to bring it forth, to see it whole, to give it form and meaning. All were enclosed in letters to my grown children.

I want to thank my husband and children for the depth and purpose they have given to my life, for the emotions they have released, and for the encouragement they have given me to develop whatever talents I have. I thank them and my friends for listening to me, for laughing and crying with me, and for urging publication.

The recurring *I* in these poems is embarrassing but inevitable. I speak only for myself, with the hope that the experiences are so universal that *you* will become the *I* as you read them.

Thanks to Reinhold Kaebitzsch and Walter Ettl for their advice on publishing, to Audrey Walsh, Nancy Stroud, Marylinn Berntsen, Marilyn Everitt, and Carol Brady for their editorial help. Special thanks to Roberta Froncek for the sketches, and to Tad Froncek for putting it all together.

Genevieve Smith Whitford

To my children,
and their children.

Queen Anne's Lace

Did I tell you about Queen Anne's lace
when you were children?
And Jack-in-the-pulpits
and anemone?
My mother told me.
I tried to plant ideas in you
and they took root and grew,
but ideas are a means to an end.
Queen Anne's lace is an end in itself,
a presence,
a reassurance,
a statement beyond dispute.
I *hope* I remembered
to tell you about
Queen Anne's lace.

Another Day

I turn, stretch, and open my eyes
to another day,
not so kaleidoscopic as the dream,
not so ordered as the book
that put me to sleep,
but consequential,
each act pivotal.
Life wavers on a choice, a step,
a turn of the wheel to avoid collision.
I will survive by reason,
dumb luck, or grace of God.
I know but one thing of this day:
that I will rise to meet it.

Eventide

At eventide, we feel the pall
of seas we did not sail, of all
the shells unnoticed on the shore,
of sunlight past our shuttered door,
of work undone, of dreams inept,
of songs unsung, of kindness kept.
How can I conquer lethargy?
Tear open eyes were meant to see?
Unclasp hands to wrest from time
the precious gifts that could be mine?

A Square Peg

Some there are who sew and cook.
I like to eat, I like to look
at recipe and pattern book.
I *want* to please my spouse and friends;
I'd like, sometime, to meet the ends.
I try, I try, but always fate
or indolence doth make me late.
Whene'er I start, the phone doth ring,
or I go out to meet the spring,
or else I lack the vital thing
to put it all together.
It falls apart or fails to jell,
or scorches when I miss the bell.
It takes a patience I have not,
a mind for measure, time and plot.
Efficiency is sure the key,
so, pray, where is a place for me,
who majored in philosophy?

The Woman Poet

The poet in her struggles
to be free.
A yearning in her womb,
a certain loneliness,
have led to open-ended,
unrelenting commitment.
She is trapped in the playpen,
bound by the demands
and limitations
of a family.
The tug at breast
of suckling babe
brings some reward,
but she cries,
and her tears transfuse
to guilt.
She dreams of an empty space,
where people enter,
one by one,
to stimulate the mind
or excite the passions,
and then leave,
at her bidding.
She needs a quiet place
to meditate, to assimilate, to translate
life into words.

But the woman in her knows
that words are a substitute
for life.
Let her child sicken unto death
and she would sell her soul,
her talent,
all her written words
for this unspoken,
living, breathing affirmation
of life.

Rage

*Be still, you will
destroy yourself
with rage,* he said.
But I must cry
and beat the wall
or I am dead.

Amniocentesis

I tremble at the thought
of an amniocentesis,
not fearing for myself so much
as feeling we betray the child
by this invasion
of his private waters,
where sloughed off cells,
like tea leaves in a cup,
may count against him
as scientific seers
read his fate
in microscopic smear.

Sonic waves,
refracted by my unborn babe,
trace his image on a screen.
Knowing where to probe,
the needle will not scar
his tender flesh
as it extracts a portion
of the amniotic fluid
already marked by his unique
and predetermined genes.

I see a wisp
of flesh and bone
floating upon the screen,
the budding limbs in motion
though we count his age
in weeks.
How big is my baby? I ask,
and the doctor replies,
About the size of a sparrow.

Now I wait to know
the child has all his parts,
and can cope,
I hope,
with life's exigencies.
And every sparrow that I see
quickens the sense of life
that grows in me.

Post-Amniocentesis

No question,
at the birth,
of sex,
deformity.
This child comes
complete
with warranty.

From the Kitchen Door

I've not gone far from my kitchen door,
(the nursery is but a step or more)
but I have seen love, in its shining grace,
and hatred on the self-same face.
War and peace and trade and more,
all abound on my kitchen floor.
Tears and laughter, work and play
tangle my footsteps every day.
Some of drudgery, some of pain,
much I could not do again,
but this is life, and life is good . . .
I would not change it if I could.

My Family

Sometimes they are the enemy,
sometimes they are my love.
Most times, at the same time,
they are both of the above.

Expiation

When I was small
I thought no one
was loved so much as I
because
no one else
had my mother.

Then one day I said,
beneath my breath,
I hate you
and I thought no one
was cursed as I with guilt.

When I had a child
I thought no one
was blessed as I
with this near perfect
child.

Then one day
she looked at me
with eyes that said,
I hate you and
I knew my love
had made her strong
and free,
and knowing this,
the guilt
went out of me.

Night Watch

I am taut,
suspended,
wanting sleep
but wide awake,
waiting for
the sound of you.
It is irrational,
but I can neither
cancel fear
of the unknown,
nor yet concede
that you are now
a man.

Moving

We, who have been uprooted many times,
have moved again.
We have packed up our children and our goods,
and shut beloved doors.
We have wrapped our hopes and plans
in strong boxes,
and dragged them across the land
to plant in new soil.
We have survived.
We bud anew,
growing into the corners
of this other house and town,
pruned and fertilized.

This Is Home

This is home to me now.
As I cross the town,
houses fit into the crannies
of my recollection.
My mind flows around them
to the curve of the road
and the trees beyond.
My knowing and their being coincide.
I am content.

Hickory Nuts

Hickory nuts? In a store?
I thought you had to hunt them in the woods.
And shelled?
I thought it took cousins
around the kitchen table
to pry them from their shells.
I carry them home triumphantly,
transported from city sights and sounds
to the country I knew as a child,
and to Aunt Beth's hickory nut cake,
which I will bake for my children,
hoping they will taste in it
a simpler time . . . .
when nuts fell from trees
and eggs came from nests
and sugar poured from bins
and cream thickened on the pantry shelf,
and when blended together,
could not be dehydrated or packaged or sold,
but given to your family,
with love.

Bermuda

Out of Season and Thirty Years Late

Clouds hang low and winds are cool,
we suffer in the heated pool.
We scorn the bikes and ride the ferry,
sip our punch and eat the cherry.
Love's polite instead of passioned,
(after fifty, sex is rationed)
but where else would better be
than ivory sands beside the sea?
Come, take my hand and walk with me.

Biopsy

Dark knot of fear,
encapsulated,
hidden deep within
the healthy tissue
of our hope,
but there
until the scalpel probes
and microscope affirms
that life,
not death,
prevails.

A Mother's Grief

Close the eyes
that no longer see,
cover the face
that will never again
smile back at me,
wrap the body,
take it away,
but *he* will stay with me.
I'll draw him back
into myself,
a swelling burden
that will press upon
my flesh and bone
and make me cry,
cry with a pain
that won't be eased
by hours of labor,
but by years
of caring
for the living.

Plaint

Now that I know
that love is enough
for mothering,
no need to wonder, worry,
if you love,
they have grown from my arms.

Now that I've learned
to listen to
their childish talk
without straining toward
bigger, worldlier voices,
they are done with telling.

Now that I know
that adolescent arrogance
is only the hopeful boast
that *I will be a better man*
and build a better world!
they are gone from home.

The Ache

Oh, the ache when children go!
I feel a loss of vital flow,
regardless of the truth I know,
that they must leave if they're to grow.

Neville's Gate

Fence the yard,
if fence you must,
to keep the dogs from straying,
but leave a gate
that opens wide
to welcome children playing.

Gray September Day

On a gray September day
we drive away
from our last child,
standing uncertainly
on a strange college campus,
waving good-bye
to his childhood
and his family.
There is a wrench
and rush of tears
as this last cord is cut,
another one of life's connections
broken,
leaving us weakened
and detached.

Now we move in new directions,
following our interests,
developing our talents,
remembering what we were
before we had children,
for now we are all of that
and more.

Autumn Sun

The autumn sun
fills our empty rooms
with warmth and light.
We stretch ourselves,
free to roam and grow,
no longer caught
in the clutter and distraction
of domesticity.
We are strong and confident
as never before,
now that our children are grown
in competence and wisdom
beyond our expectations,
multiplying our hopes,
extending our dreams,
returning our love.
Now there is time
to develop old talents,
to renew old friendships,
to revive old passions,
to discover new interests.
As leaf colors with seeding done,
so may we glow in autumn sun.

Who Am I?

Who am I?
At sixty, I still ask.
First, child of loving parents.
Carry me, Daddy!
I remember saying it
in Christmas rush
on State Street in Chicago
when I was very small,
and he lifted me
and I rested in his arms.

I wailed again
when Mother left the house,
but Daddy said,
Be a good girl
and we will bring you
a baby brother,
and they did.

Babe no more,
I am a sister now.
I bask in his cherubic smile
and try to hold his round softness
in my thin arms.

And then he grows
and tortures me.
In innocence,
he blinds my doll
and spoils my game.
I become a bad girl.
How can you be mean
to your very own brother?
says my mother.

And then to school.
I am a good reader,
a painful conscience,
a wonderer.
Where do babies come from?
Who is God?
What does it mean?

In high school
and in college,
I am a student,
but not a scholar,
a harpist,
but not a musician,
an actor,
but not a star,
an editor,
but not a writer,
an also ran.

I graduate, and rush into the arms
of him who says,
You are an angel!
But what do angels know
of getting meals
and scrubbing floors?

You are pregnant,
says the doctor.
I walk home on clouds
and then begin to retch.
I am all body,
resisting,
releasing,
and then becoming
a mother.

She is my all now,
but where am I?
No matter.
No time.
I suckle her, then worry
lest the milk run dry.
I want the best for her,
but where am I?
Lost in diapers
and Little League
and P.T.A.

This, too, will pass
and we will say good-bye
to graduates
and travelers
and unsuspecting brides.

They are all gone.
Our empty arms
embrace grandchildren now.
But who is this
who teaches them
to Patty Cake
and Peek-a-Boo?
Surely my mother,
or her mother before her.
They are the same songs,
the same gestures,
the same games.
Automatically,
they come from me.

I see it now.
I am a shell.
I grow and calcify.
Cells divide within me,
ideas evolve,
but nothing is permanent,
nothing new . . .
I am a temporary source
of life flow,
of ideas,
of traditions;
a vessel
to contain,
to nurture,
to pour forth.

I dandle the latest baby
on my knee.
Trot, trot to Boston
to buy a loaf of bread.
Trot, trot back again,
the old trot's dead!

Don't cry!
The wine of life flows on,
from yeasty depths
of each succeeding generation,
in quality and color
of infinite variation,
distilled in me,
absorbed by you
in life's brief celebration.

Continuum

I do not mean
to smother you
with gifts,
nor hurt your pride,
nor yet diminish you.
These are not gifts at all . . .
a dinner out,
a simple dress,
a bassinette . . .
but continuum
of father's arm,
of mother's breast,
of Santa's myth.
The warmth,
the food,
the shelter,
come from us
in small ways now,
a tapering of
the elemental urge
to help the young.
Take freely from us
while we have to give,
as you are giving freely
to your own.

Celebration

We gather round the table
to celebrate another birthday.
It is her grandmother's table,
transported across the country
to this new home of hers.
We could be thousands of miles
and generations away,
so much it evokes
of birthdays past.
Only the faces change.
Her children light the candles now,
and proudly bear the cake.
Her husband sits at the head of the table
as we, her parents, newly grand,
move aside to celebrate
on-going life.

A Visit To Grandmother

When you come, her arms will reach out
to hold you close for a while.
She will have made up your father's bed for you,
and brought out the old worn blocks.
She will play Animal Lotto with you,
and read Ferdinand and Winnie the Pooh.
And when you go, she will cry
because she knows the child she loves
will never come again.
Another year and he will have grown
further into the man he is to be,
and though she will love him more,
today she is bereaved.

To My Spouse

You are not my better half,
nor I, yours,
but yet a part of me,
a left hand,
(I am right handed)
which brings me the stuff of life,
holds it steady while I shape it.
I am *your* left hand,
opening doors for you to enter.
Another could not do as well,
without our shared intent
and long experience.
There is, in marriage,
an exchange of mind and muscle,
a curious balance,
often precarious,
sometimes perfect.
For forty years, we have shifted weights
as we centered into life.
I feel stronger in marriage
than before,
and stronger each year
than the last.
Do you?

To My Sons

Thank you, my sons,
for being masculine,
for being courageous and strong,
(who says women are not?)
yet gentle and loving.
Thank you for your determination
to develop your minds,
your bodies,
and your talents,
and to put them to good use.
Thank you for wanting
to father children,
to carry them on your shoulders,
and to teach them responsibility
by example.
Thank you for caring about
truth and beauty and justice.
They are as fragile as children.
They need your strength
and your will
to survive.

To My Daughters

Thank you, my daughters
for being feminine,
for wanting children,
for nursing babies,
(and spreading the word),
for being relaxed and loving
with your families,
but losing patience sometimes,
relieving me of the guilt I felt
when I couldn't cope with you.
Thank you for caring about your homes,
and for teaching me to use bright colors
and natural foods.
Thank you for being resourceful
and creative,
and for honing your intuitive minds
with an enlightened intelligence.
Thank you for being concerned
about the world,
but willing to stay home
while your children are young.
Thank you for giving
to family and friends,
but reserving some energy
for growing.
You are doing better than I
with your children
and your lives,
which makes me think
that I did something right,
after all.

To A Young Mother

Don't be dismayed
by a smile on the face
of an older woman
when your child
misbehaves.
She is not critical
or smug.
She smiles because
she has been through
all of this
and more,
and has survived.

Patience

Don't fret about the weeds.
Someday the rains will come,
and after that,
the earth will yield them freely,
if you are there to pull.

Don't fret about a frown
on the face of one you love.
That dark mood will pass
and some light word
will bring a smile,
if you are there to speak.

Reunion

We sat talking
in the summer sun,
lazing on the swing
and as it swung,
we moved from light to shadow,
weaving strands
of memories and plans.
And so we added length
and strength and color
from the varied fiber
of our lives,
knowing that the parts
may fray and ravel,
but the fabric
of our family
survives.

Ceremony

Why am I moved
by this that once I scorned . . .
the somber robes,
the measured steps,
the high flown words,
the solemn invocation?
Ceremony.
Once it stifled me,
appeared to be
impediment to growth.
Now I see
that it enlarges,
adds to life's expectancy.
I join the slow procession,
from past to present to future,
and find identity
of pulse and purpose
in the anonymity
of flowing robes.
I rise to the podium,
hold the scepter high,
hear my unformed words
crystalize on microphonic waves,
and dedicate myself anew
to man's old aspirations.

Found In The Metropolitan

The children of Jacob Schiff,
carved in marble, bas relief,
by St. Gaudens in 1907.
A boy and girl, holding hands,
their handsome dog in tow.
Banker Schiff, knowing that his vaults of gold
could not keep his children
young and beautiful forever,
commissioned them to be
immortalized in stone,
and with them, *my* children,
starched and combed,
their rivalries forgotten,
their mongrel dogs
transposed by memory
into wolf-hounds.

Travel Pictures

On a dark night in Switzerland,
white swans on a black lake.

On a clear, bright day in Mykonos,
a white cat on the white cobblestones
of a street of whitewashed houses.

On a cold November day,
a red rose, blooming unexpectedly
in the snow
in the garden at Malmaison,
where Josephine waited for Napoleon.

There is the Parthenon,
the Taj Mahal,
and Machu Pichu, the lost city of the Incas,
but their pictures blur
in memory.
It takes some well known living thing
to bring them into focus.
It is not the gargoyles of Notre Dame
that link us to another time and place,
but the cats who beg for food
in the Colosseum in Rome.

On Leaving Palm Springs

Let me take one last draught
of desert sun
and mountain view,
and try to hold,
in my mind's eye,
a crown of palm
without the scaley trunk
and withered frond.
I'll turn away
from rubble hills,
shake free of prickly bush
and rock and sand,
give one last burp
of Bernaise sauce and wine,
peel away my forced
convention smile,
and turn, relieved,
toward home.

Winter Flight

From high above, the great mid-west
seems locked in snow.
There is no sign of life,
but this I know:
at intersections of the roads and fields
are homes, and in them,
light and fire and human warmth.
The stillness of apparent hibernation
is but delusion.
Each day, the baby wakes,
the children are sent off to school,
the mother cleans and bakes,
the farmer milks his cows
and mends the fences.
Underground, the seed sleeps;
above ground, the rabbit and the farmer
struggle to survive.
High above the land
we fly from west to east,
telescoping time into an early night,
seeming to see far
but knowing there is more
than we can ever see.

The Stewardess

Lady of the aisle,
are you plastic
as your smile,
and as the tray you bear?
Or is there knife within you
whose serreated edge
is of strong steel,
to carve through more
than Tuesday's meal?
Do you see past
the blackened lash
and painted lid,
beyond this seat
you've labeled
occupied?
On your off day
do you brush away
the lacquer spray
that holds each hair
in place?
I hope somewhere
you're free
to scream and cry
and shout obscenity!
On high, you are reduced
to prate of coffee,
tea or juice.
I mourn for you
who sell the right
to be yourself,
as stewardess in flight.

At The Shore

People sprawl
in their debris,
limbs clotted
with sweat and sand,
eyes closed
against the sun.

Gulls soar
in the air
with grace
and purpose
and unfailing sense
of direction.

Souvenir

Buy what you will
of arts and crafts
in that exotic store.
It will look paltry
by the shell
I found upon the shore.

Class Reunion

We start the day with raspberries,
extravagant pleasure
on a cold October morning.
They are full and ripe
and he says, as he tastes them,
This is as near as I've ever been
to heaven!
I remind him that he has often said as much
to me,
and we laugh together.
We are happier today,
having raspberries,
out of season,
at the Union League Club in Chicago,
than we were when he was working
his way through college,
and I was worried
about the next exam,
and neither of us knew
who we were
or where we were going.

Today, we are going
to a class reunion,
to look for familiar faces
beneath the puffy eyes
and sagging cheeks
of classmates
whom we never really knew,
because forty years ago
we hardly knew ourselves.
We are all larger than life now,
with accomplishments wrapped round us
in layers,
and we display our children
and grandchildren
like jewels.
We congratulate each other
on surviving,
then return, with relief,
to the quiet of our room.
In the morning,
there are raspberries again,
to savor on the long trip
home.

Witness

I go alone to the pool,
but I am not alone.
I struggle with the young amputee
as he mounts the unsubstantial chair,
settles his stump on the hot plastic strips,
places the prosthesis within reach,
and turns the empty sockets of his eyes
toward the sun and the pool.
With him, I sense the coming
of a lumpish woman
who spills out of her tight jeans
and settles beside him.
She trails long red nails
through her bleached hair
and talks softly to her man.
He is her man,
though many parts are missing.
The heavy service ring,
the Braille watch,
weight his good arm with gold.
With her, I reach for the other hand
and try to erase the ridges of his scar.
I am, within the hour,
man, woman, old, young,
fat, thin, maimed, restored.
There is no other one.

Cousin Cathy, Once Removed

She lay there old, frail,
the last of her family,
with no one to care but grand nieces
and cousins once removed.
A golden sea of grain
waved in the summer sun
beyond the window of the Home.
We spoke of Willa Cather.
She was a link between
our disparate age and situation.
Through Antonia, I too had experienced
ripening wheat and changing seasons
and pioneering self-sufficiency.
Through Willa Cather, and others,
she had lived
beyond the boundaries of her village,
and more than her ninety years.
I marveled at her memory
and came another day to talk to her,
but she was gone.
The bed was empty, bare.
No imprint of her fragile frame
remained on the smooth, cold sheet.
Still, beyond the window
waved the field of yellow grain,
soon to feel the reapers blade,
but sure to grow again.

Riding Toward Death On a Clear Day

What is this wild terrain of barren peaks?
My world?
I never thought to ride so high
and see so clear
   veins of rivers,
   ribboned roads,
   flecks of brush
   on rocky soil.
The hills wear down to sand.
My land
becomes a desert waste.
Circles appear, and then the square.
What geometry is carved on prairie?
Great fields, plotted of lines and curves.
Man works with arcs and angles;
nature flows.

Now a valley feathers out
from some dry river bed,
and then earth settles in a blend
of fields and trees.
A city grows from houses
pressed together on the streets.
The runway rushes past
and with a lurch, we face
reality.

Now man looms large.
He blocks my way,
for he has deadlines too . . .
but mine's with death.
It blurs her eyes
and stills her tongue,
but I must hurry there
to catch her tear,
for she is old
and I am young,
until she dies . . .
then I am old instead.

Immortality

Mother, you have joined the angels now,
left your withered flesh,
your faltered step,
the deaf ear,
the tongue that no longer spoke for you.
In our hearts and minds
you are restored.
You stand tall again
and your voice is clear.
We recollect the love you gave,
the force you were,
the strength we have derived from you.
With our tears we baptize you
and give you immortality.

Reflection

I passed a mirror recently
and saw my mother there.
She seemed surprised to see me . . .
I'd caught her unaware.
But there's no mistake about it.
The dewlaps and graying hair
are so familiar to me,
I'd know them anywhere!

With Age

Self is less demanding,
the mind breaks free,
reaching for
and sometimes touching
universality.

Brittle Boughs

The Christmas greens
go up in flame,
their brittle boughs
to light a New Year's fire.
Burst of warmth and beauty,
in a moment gone . . .
better than to drop
dry holly berries
one by one.

Midnight

The minute hand moves,
relentlessly,
toward the midnight
of my sixty-fifth year.
How can I be old
and yet feel young?
I've just begun to live!
I'm still learning how
to run a house,
to cook a meal,
to manage a family,
to control my emotions,
to play the harp,
to write poetry.
Even at this moment,
which startles me
into awareness,
the writing of a poem
seems more important
than the ticking
of the clock.

The Sense Of Wonder

They say all things are wonderous
to a child;
I say the sense of wonder
grows with age.
The child accepts the faceless voice
that speaks through telephones,
takes moon walk in his stride,
nor doubts that man can fly
in winged machines.
He knows the sun will rise,
that spring will come
and seeds will bud and bloom,
assuming that they bear their fruit
for him.
He takes for granted fugues and virtuosos,
and counts cathedral spire
no greater than his tower of blocks,
while I watch, with awe and wonder,
the flight of a bird,
the birth of a child,
the growth of a tree,
the faith of man
that conquers pain
with hope and charity.

Each day brings new possibilities.
Each day I see further into the universe,
deeper into the heart.
Each day I discover new relationships,
between the flower and the child,
between the present and the past,
between the whole and the part,
between myself and others.
The child asks why
and then forgets to listen.
The adult listens
without knowing why.

When I Am Old

Don't look down on me,
for I have stood tall.
Don't speak for me;
I have not lost my will.
Don't talk behind my back;
I hear more than you know.
Don't laugh at this old flesh;
there is a young spirit inside.
Be patient while I move aside
for you to rush by.
Keep your balance
lest you fall
before your time.

So Let It Be

Let me die peacefully
in my own bed,
when work is done
and children raised
and my full share
of tears and laughter
spent.
The accident,
the firey death
are an abbreviation.
I want to write
The End to life,
though hand grows weak
and letters dim.

I have watched the old die.
There comes a time when,
face to wall
and food untouched,
they choose to sleep.
So let it be
with me.